Christina Does Yoga

Mona Sabah

A "Go & Make Disciples of All Nations!" Series Book

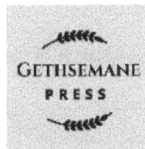

GETHSEMANE
PRESS

DEDICATION

This book is dedicated to my lovely children and grandchildren. May you walk with the Lord humbly and shine the light of Christ all the days of your life.

I also dedicate this to my church family. Thank you for the love you have for Christ and for one another. May the Lord help us to proclaim that we are saved by grace alone, through faith alone, in Christ alone, as revealed by Scripture alone, to the glory of God alone.

TO THE READER:

1 Peter 3:15 (ESV) says, "But in your hearts revere Christ as Lord. Always be prepared to give an answer to everyone who asks you to give the reason for the hope that you have. But do this with gentleness and respect." This is a verse that should motivate all Christians to prepare to give answers in defense of their faith. Evangelism means to Share the Good News of the Gospel. Many times, Evangelism and Defending the Faith (Apologetics) go hand in hand.

This book is to help you talk to people from other cultures and to share the Gospel. It is meant for all ages from 1 to 100 years old. I have provided a list of Bible verses used in the book. Also, there's an easy to way to explain the Gospel towards the end of the book (Gospel Arrows). I hope these tools and the conversation between the characters in this book will equip you and the child in your life to make disciples for Jesus Christ.

In this book, Christina is introduced to Yoga by her PE teacher at school. Her History teacher, Mr. Luther helps to give Christina an understanding of Yoga's roots, spirituality, and differences between Hinduism and Christianity. There are ideas presented throughout that can help spark discussion with your child

In this series, Christina represents a Christian who meets others who are different from her. Join her as she learns about their culture and religion. See how understanding the culture can help reach new people in her life who do not know the beauty of the Gospel.

"Namaste, Class! I'm Ms. Brittany and I will be teaching you about Yoga!

Christina asked, "Ms. Brittany, that word 'Namaste' sounds funny. What does it mean?"

क ka [kʌ]	ख kha [kʰʌ]	ग ga [gʌ]	घ gha [gɦʌ]	ङ ṅa [ŋʌ]
च ca [cʌ]	छ cha [cʰʌ]	ज ja [ɟʌ]	झ jha [ɟɦʌ]	ञ ña [ɲʌ]
ट ṭa [ʈʌ]	ठ ṭha [ʈʰʌ]	ड ḍa [ɖʌ]	ढ ḍha [ɖɦʌ]	ण ṇa [ɳʌ]
त ta [t̪ʌ]	थ tha [t̪ʰʌ]	द da [d̪ʌ]	ध dha [d̪ɦʌ]	न na [nʌ]
प pa [pʌ]	फ pha [pʰʌ]	ब ba [bʌ]	भ bha [bɦʌ]	म ma [mʌ]
य ya [jʌ]	र ra [rʌ]	ल la [lʌ]	व va [ʋʌ]	
श śa [ɕʌ]	ष ṣa [ʂʌ]	स sa [sʌ]		
ह ha [ɦʌ]	ळ ḷa [ɭʌ]			

योग
YOGA

Mudhumita1052 cc-by-sa-4.0

Ms. Brittany said "That's a good question, Christina! Namaste is a way to greet others and to start Yoga in Sanskrit [sahn sk rit], the ancient language of India.

"When you say Namaste, you are saying 'the god in me bows to the god in you.'
"Last summer I got a scholarship as a PE teacher to a Hindu Ashram [ah sh raam] to learn Yoga so I could teach all of you.

"An Ashram is a school where people go to learn about the culture and history of Yoga.
Did you know that Yoga means 'to bind, merge or unite (yoke) together?'

"This year, I will teach you more about Yoga, mindfulness, culture, Sanskrit words and all kinds of wonderful things.

"These words come from the Bhagavad Gita [bha gah vod gee tah] – the oldest Sanskrit storybook on Yoga.

"Asana is the first word you need to know. It is the 'seat' or the pose that brings your body and mind together for meditation (koinonia.org.ua).

"The words mean 'I sit to unite. I welcome the yoke.' The sitting pose called the 'Lotus' position.

"We will say 'OM' while we are doing these poses so you can hear vibration in your throat. This is the sound frequency found in nature and you can unite your mind, body and spirit with the universe.

AUM
"OM"

"3 Letters A-U-M unites also with the sound of the Trimurti (3 gods): Brahma (A), Vishnu (U) and Shiva (M) (Yogabasics.com/practice/yogaforbeginners /yoga-symbols).

"Mantra [mon trah] means sounds or words that we will sing, speak and repeat for meditation on self-love and happiness.

"I found a few of these to share with you:

You yourself, as much as anybody in the entire universe, deserve your love and affection. -Buddha

You become what you believe.
–Oprah Winfrey

Think happy thoughts. –Peter Pan

It is inner stillness that will save and transform the world. -Eckhart Tolle

Do not dwell in the past, do not dream of the future, concentrate the mind on the present moment. -Buddha

"Meditation is another thing we will do every time in Yoga class.

YOGA MEDITATION:
a way to focus thoughts on the god
inside you or on other objects

BREATHING:

MINDFULNESS:

MANTRA:

DO NOTHING:

FOCUS:

monsabahbooks.com

"We will empty our minds and fill them up with mantras about loving yourself!

"Prana [prah nah] means 'Life Force' or the energy in everything. Through mindful breathing in each nostril, we will control the Prana. We will practice this in our meditation exercises.

"Savasana [sah vah sahna] 'Corpse Pose' is done last to indicate death. We will lay down absolutely still and not move a muscle. Then we curl up like a baby into the fetal position, (rebirth in Yoga).

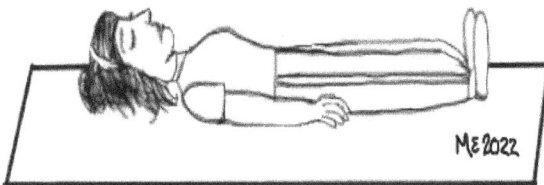

"Shanti [shon tee] means peace.

Chakra: 7 Wheels = Centers of Spiritual Energy

"Chakras [chock rahs] are energy centers in your body. The flag of India has a Chakra wheel in the center, as a symbol of the Hindu Religion. Yoga is a way you can get inner peace or shanti by lining up the 7 chakras inside you.

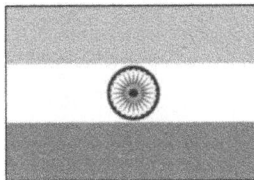

"We will begin and end each class with the Mudra [moo drah]. It is a gesture of joined hands. We will touch our heart since it is the gateway to our inside. This way, we will engage your heart, mind, and body in the practice of Yoga."

Chand crossed her arms and interrupted the class by saying, "Excuse me, Ms. Brittany. I am a Muslim and we are not allowed to do anything that has to do with Hinduism."

Ms. Brittany answered, "Chand, this has nothing to do with Hinduism or religion."

Chand questioned, "Well, why are these words all from Sanskrit and you were talking about Hindu stuff?"

Ms. Brittany said, "Chand, Yoga was created in India by Hindus, so it uses these words.

"But we are just doing this for exercise and fun! Don't worry about it so much!"

Chand asked again, "Ms. Brittany, if it's okay, I don't want to do it because you were saying 'there is a god in me bowing to a god in you.' Isn't that idol worship?"

Ms. Brittany shook her head and said, "Chand, if you have a problem with it, just go to the Office until class is finished."

Ms. Brittany turned back to the class and said, "Let's do some Sun Salutation poses. These are stretches to greet the sun god as creator. Honoring the sun is an Asana called Surya Namaskar [Soo rya Nah mah scar]. 'Surya' means that the sun is 'the eye of the world." 'Nama' means to bow or salute and 'kar' means to do.

"After we bow down to the sun, let's do 'The Cobra.' This pose will help you become more flexible as you bend your spine.

ME 2022

"Shiva [shee vah], the god of destruction and Vishnu [veesh noo], the god of protection are always shown with a snake named 'Sheesha' around them. This snake glides around the sky and is a symbol of infinity.

ME 2022

"As you flex, the cobra snake energy will glide up your spine and help you to be strong!

"Another pose for being strong is the 'Warrior.' This pose is called the 'Virabhadrasana' [veera bha drah + asana (pose)]. 'Virabhadra' is the bodily form of the god Shiva with a powerful Hindu warrior.

"Together, they balance strength and flexibility. That brings power to you as you channel this warrior god.

"Class is over! You did a great job learning so much today! We will do more poses next week as we study Yoga this year!"

After PE, Christina went to her History class with Mr. Luther. He noticed she was distracted during the whole hour.

After class, Mr. Luther asked her what was wrong.

She told him, "I learned Yoga in PE today. I'm confused because the teacher kept talking about Hinduism.

"In Sunday School, my teacher taught us the 10 Commandments.

"The first and second commandments tell us to worship God alone and not to have any idols.

"Mr. Luther, don't the Hindu people worship many idols?"

Mr. Luther smiled and replied, "Christina, I'm so glad you are talking to me about this. I have taught the 10 Commandments at my church. Exodus 20 states that the first commandment is,

'You shall have no other gods before me (Exo 20:3).'

"The second commandment is, 'You shall not make for yourself a carved image, or any likeness of anything that is in heaven above, or that is in the earth beneath, or that is in the water under the earth (Exo 20:4).' Both commands tell us to be careful and always put God first.

"Now, let's talk about Hinduism. Many false religions have come out of this belief system. Hindus worship over 330 million gods.

"Their religious book is called the 'Bhagavad Gita.' It explains stories of false gods. I think it is important for you to know that in the Gita, Yoga is mentioned over 100 times as worship to these idols (www.worldhistory.org).

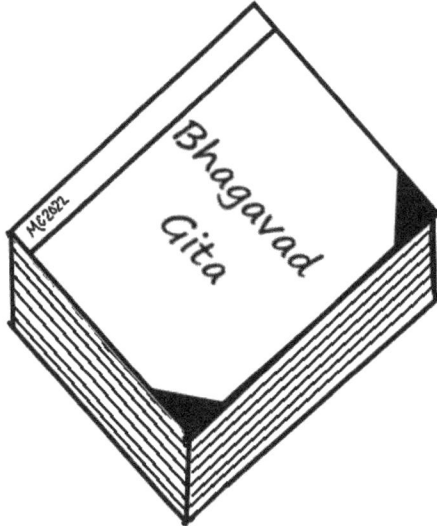

"Yoga is a spiritual pathway that Hindus use to follow their gods. The way they do this is to focus on themselves; essentially, they are worshiping themselves."

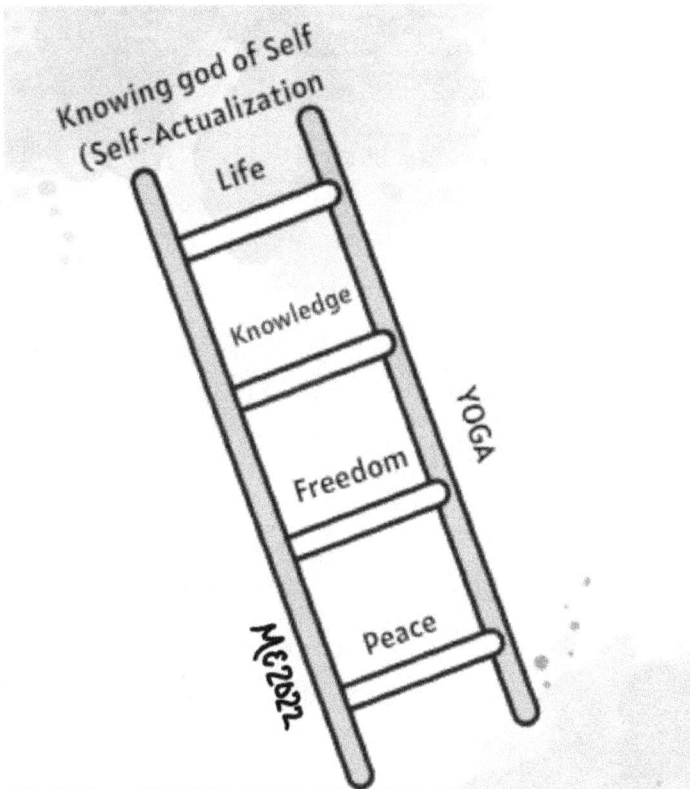

Christina was thinking about all this and asked, "So is it okay for a Christian to do Yoga?"

Mr. Luther replied, "It's common for people to use Yoga as an exercise. What they don't know is that this is a form of Hindu worship and focuses the mind on Hindu gods through the positions that represent the different gods.

"As Christians, we are to worship God in Spirit and truth (John 4:24)."

Christina asked, "Is there a type of Yoga for Christians? Wait... Mr. Luther, doesn't Ms. Brittany teach a Christian Yoga class at her church?"

Mr. Luther said, "Just because something says 'Christian' or takes place at a church does not mean it's something the Bible says is okay to do. In the Bible, God is very specific about what He accepts as worship.

"Christina, we need to test everything against the Word of God. 'Now these Jews were more noble than those in Thessalonica; they received the word with all eagerness, examining the Scriptures daily to see if these things were so (Acts 17:11).'

"Let's look together at some of the things in Yoga.

"First, Yoga means 'to be yoked' – that means to unite the mind with the poses of different gods, or of nature, or of meditations (mantras).

MSE 2022

"Many people call Yoga 'Devotion in Motion.'

"Second, if you are focused on these, you cannot focus on Christ.

"There are lots of verses in the Bible that talk about what we should meditate on, like Joshua 1:8, Psalm 1:2, 40:8, 119:11, 119:115, 119:97 (all of Psalm 119, really).

"Yoga claims to clear the mind. However, the Lord has promised to renew our mind through His word. Romans 12:2 says, 'Do not be conformed to this world, but be transformed by the renewal of your mind, that by testing you may discern what is the will of God, what is good and acceptable and perfect.' Our minds are not renewed by emptying them or by our own power, but only by the power of the Holy Spirit who works in believers."

Christina looked up a few of the verses in the Bible her teacher had on his desk and she said, "I see what you are saying, Mr. Luther.

"We did several poses today, including the Cobra and the Warrior pose.

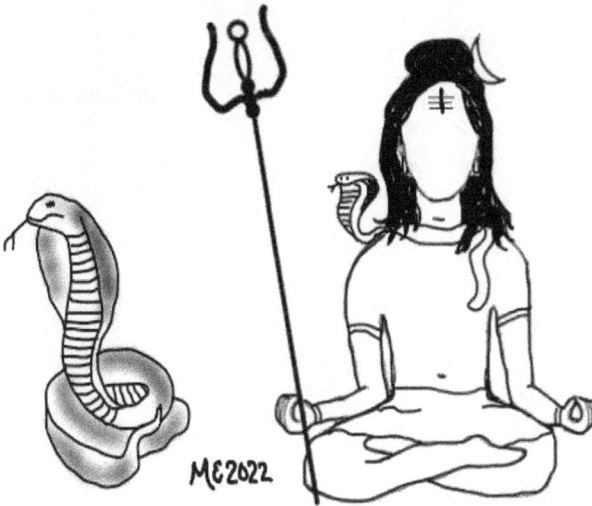

"The first pose reminded me of the snake in the Garden of Eden.

"The Warrior pose was weird because Ms. Brittany talked a lot about a Hindu god whose name was The Destroyer."

Mr. Luther looked concerned and said, "Hmm... The Snake and The Destroyer?

"What do they have in common, Christina?"

Christina answered, "Well, do they have something to do with Satan?"

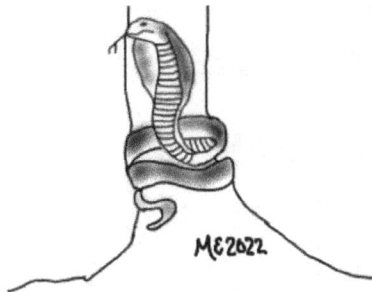

Mr. Luther said, "Very good! The Bible calls Satan BOTH of those names.

Genesis
Serpent

Revelation
Ancient
Serpent
Destroyer

ME2022

"The book of Genesis has several verses you might want to look up: Genesis 3:1 and 3:14. The Book of Revelation calls Satan the 'ancient serpent' (Rev 12:9).

"Isaiah 33:1, John 10:10, and Revelation 9:11 call Satan the destroyer 'who only comes to steal, kill, and destroy.'

"As Christians, we believe only in Jesus Christ for giving us peace, strength, and new life through His death and resurrection on the cross.

"Acts 4:12 states, 'And there is salvation in no one else, for there is no other name under heaven given among men by which we

must be saved.' Jesus is the only One who saves us from destruction. He alone does the saving – not us. Every bit of Hinduism and Yoga are works.

"So, tell me Christina, is Ms. Brittany doing yoga next week in your exercise class?"

Christina replied, "Yes, I think Ms. Brittany said we are doing this all year.

"You know what? Chand was allowed to sit out today because she said Muslims don't do Yoga. Should I ask to sit out too?"

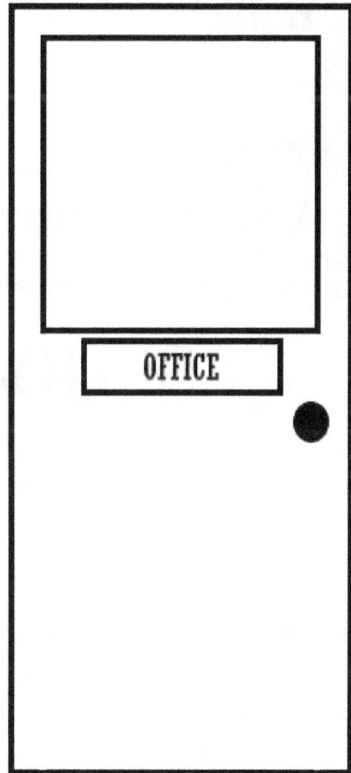

Mr. Luther answered, "Christina, just as Chand was allowed to sit out because of her beliefs, you also have the right to sit out and not do Yoga because of your beliefs.

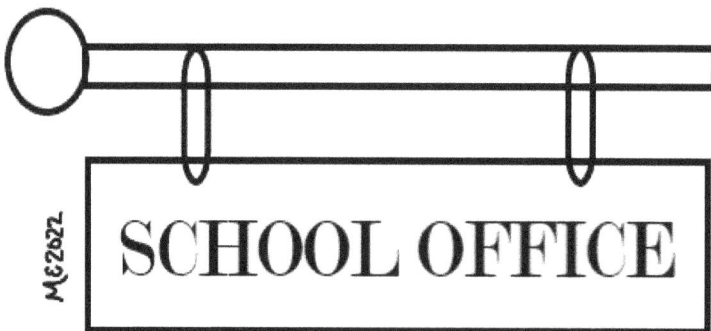

SCHOOL OFFICE

"If you know that something goes against the Bible, you should respectfully ask to be excused from participating.

"Maybe you can talk to your mom about this and she can help you.

ME 2022

"That way, you can pray for those who might be confused and don't know that Jesus, our Lord and Savior said, 'I am the way, and the truth, and the life. No one comes to the Father except through me (John 14:6).'"

Christina agreed to talk to her mom and said, "Thank you for explaining that Yoga is how Hindus pray to millions of gods.

"Now I can explain this to my Sunday School class and help my friends to know what to do!"

PRAYER

Lord, we thank You for your beautiful Word the Bible, and for our salvation through Christ alone. You tell us that Your yoke is easy because Your burden is light (Matthew 11:30). Please help us to remember and obey Your commandments. Help us to pray and seek wisdom from Christians who love You and love Your Word. We thank You for our church family and spiritual leaders. We pray for You to guide us so we can honor You in all we do. Your word is a lamp to our feet and a light to our path (Psalm 119:105). In the name of Jesus, we ask. Amen.

Note to the Reader

This book addresses the very real situation of classes in both public and private schools that are introducing Yoga as a regular part of the curriculum for exercise and study. While the secular world does not see any harm in this, there is a very real issue that faces our children. Schools are taking out religion, yet they are bringing in other forms of religious worship. Some people are aware of this but others are unaware of the subtle ways this can impact our culture and families. The amount of government funding for Yoga in schools is growing annually across the nation.

When I was growing up as a Muslim in the United States, I was invited to several Yoga classes. It is interesting to note that as a Muslim, there was an abhorrence to anything that had to do with Hinduism and idol worship. This is the reason why Chand is clear on her belief system as a Muslim. When I was saved by Christ, I found it unbelievable that those who called themselves Christians would choose to practice Yoga – a clear form of Hindu worship. Over 35 million Americans are now practicing Yoga and it has entered into the church, repackaged as "Christian Yoga" or "Holy Yoga."

Hindu religious practices are made valid and are even elevated in the mainstream culture as a way to achieve peace and mental strength. This is NOT what the Bible teaches. We, as Christians, do not "improve upon" the Bible by adding anything to our worship.

There is a word called "SYNCRETISM." The Oxford Dictionary defines this as "the amalgamation or attempted amalgamation of different religions, cultures, or schools of thought."

We cannot mix Hinduism with Christ – no matter what the culture says. We cannot mix Hinduism with Christ, no matter how much a teacher states it's good for exercise, mental health, or relaxation.

Christians draw close to God through prayer to Him alone and by reading and meditating on the Bible, the Word of God. Mark 12:29-30 records, "Jesus answered, The most important is, 'Hear, O Israel: The Lord our God, the Lord is one. And you shall love the Lord your God with all your heart and with all your soul and with all your mind and with all your strength.'"

We need to "test the spirits" and teach our children how to do the same. 1 John 4:1 reminds us, "Beloved, do not believe every spirit, but test the spirits to see whether they are from God, for many false prophets have gone out into the world."

May this book help you and others to understand how the practice of Yoga can be an invitation into Hinduism. We cannot go as the culture goes – we are called to live in this world but be set apart for the work of God's Kingdom.

Please check out the other books with Christina & friends in the "GO & MAKE DISCIPLES OF ALL NATIONS!" Series.

BIBLE VERSES

(in order of appearance)

Exodus 20:3-4
You shall have no other gods before me. You shall not make for yourself a carved image, or any likeness of anything that is in heaven above, or that is in the earth beneath, or that is in the water under the earth.

John 4:24
God is spirit, and those who worship him must worship in spirit and truth.

Joshua 1:8
This Book of the Law shall not depart from your mouth, but you shall meditate on it day and night, so that you may be careful to do according to all that is written in it. For then you will make your way prosperous, and then you will have good success.

Psalm 1:2
…but his delight is in the law of the LORD, and on his law he meditates day and night.

Psalm 40:8
I delight to do your will, O my God: your law is within my heart.

Romans 12:2
Do not be conformed to this world, but be transformed by the renewal of your mind, that by testing you may discern what is the will of God, what is good and acceptable and perfect.

*Genesis 3:1*a
Now the serpent was more crafty than any other beast of the field that the LORD God had made.

Genesis 3:14
The LORD God said to the serpent, "Because you have done this, cursed are you above all livestock and above all beasts of the field; on your belly you shall go, and dust you shall eat all the days of your life.

Revelation 12:9
And the great dragon was thrown down, that ancient serpent, who is called the devil and Satan, the deceiver of the whole world—he was thrown down to the earth, and his angels were thrown down with him.
Isaiah 33:1
Ah, you destroyer, who yourself have not been destroyed, you traitor, whom none has betrayed! When you have ceased to destroy, you will be destroyed; and when you have finished betraying, they will betray you
John 10:10
The thief comes only to steal and kill and destroy. I came that they may have life and have it abundantly.
Rev 9:11
They have as king over them the angel of the bottomless pit. His name in Hebrew is Abaddon, and in Greek he is called Apollyon [destroyer].
Acts 4:12
And there is salvation in no one else, for there is no other name under heaven given among men by which we must be saved.
Mark 12:29-30
Jesus answered, "The most important is, 'Hear, O Israel: The Lord our God, the Lord is one. 30And you shall love the Lord your God with all your heart and with all your soul and with all your mind and with all your strength"
1John 4:1
Beloved, do not believe every spirit, but test the spirits to see whether they are from God, for many false prophets have gone out into the world.
John 14:6
Jesus said to him, "I am the way, and the truth, and the life. No one comes to the Father except through me."
Matthew 11:29-30
Take my yoke upon you, and learn from me, for I am gentle and lowly in heart, and you will find rest for your souls. For my yoke is easy, and my burden is light.
Psalm 119:105
Your word is a lamp to my feet and a light to my path.

ABOUT THE AUTHOR

Mona Sabah was born in the Middle East, lived in 5 countries & speaks 3 languages. She was a Muslim for 35 years and is now an ambassador for Christ. Mona lived in the United States for 25 years without an authentic witness to the pure Gospel.

She moved to the United States from Pakistan, lived in a Muslim community in California and then thwarted the tradition of arranged marriage by marrying an American. After the events of 9/11, she decided to delve deeper into her faith by reading the Quran and praying to Allah.

When she encountered the chapter on Jesus (Isa-Surah Maryam), she couldn't figure out why this prophet was so different. She prayed to God to give her the truth and show her the way. He pointed to One: Jesus Christ – her Lord and Savior.

She writes and speaks about her salvation and stresses the importance of sharing the Good News of Christ.

She loves to draw, paint and sketch. She was thrilled to write a children's book that would use her scribblings for the glory of God!

She prays about opportunities to share her testimony about Jesus and teach others how to share the Gospel. If you would like her to speak at your event, please contact her through her Blog: monasabahbooks.com
Social Media: @monasabahbooks

OTHER BOOKS BY MONA SABAH
From Isa to Christ
Reaching Muslims – A Christian's Guide to Islam
Half in Islam, Whole in Jesus – A Woman's Worth
Christina & Chand – A Beautiful Friendship

GOSPEL ARROWS
An Easy Way to Remember the Gospel

Man cannot work his way to God, so God came down and dwelt with us (Immanuel = Jesus)

Jesus Christ died on the cross to pay for our sins

He was buried in a tomb

After 3 days, He rose again from the dead & went up to Heaven

We need to confess our sins, repent (turn back), & trust in Jesus Christ to save us from the punishment for breaking God's laws

Jesus is coming back to judge the world & take His people to Heaven to live with Him

PEOPLE I NEED TO PRAY FOR: